AN AUTISM DIAGNOSIS MUST COME
FROM A LICENSED PROFESSIONAL

OUR MISSION:

SHARE THAT EVERY CHILD ON THE AUTISM
SPECTRUM IS UNIQUE, BUT NOT ALONE.

PROVIDE A CREATIVE OUTLET FOR AUTISTIC CHILDREN TO
LEARN ABOUT THEMSELVES.

SPREAD AUTISM AWARENESS THROUGH
RELATABLE REAL LIFE SCENARIOS TO FOSTER STRONGER
RELATIONSHIPS IN THEIR COMMUNITY.

This book is not intended as a substitute for medical advice. The reader should consult a licensed professional in matters relating to their health, particularly with respect to any symptoms that may require diagnosis or medical attention.

Publisher's Cataloging-in-Publication
(Provided by Cassidy Cataloguing Services, Inc.)
Names: Martinez, Jason, author. | Martinez, Emma, author. | Paj, Eduardo, illustrator.
Title: Sprinkles has a brother with autism / written by Jason Martinez and Emma Martinez ; illustrated by Eduardo Paj.
Description: First edition. | [Arvada, Colorado] : JEI Productions LLC, [2024] | Series: Kids spectrum stories. | Audience: Elementary school children. | Summary: Having a sibling on the Autism Spectrum can feel overwhelming. In this story, Sprinkles experiences a tough situation with her brother, Chip, and she has a heart-to-heart discussion with her mother. With her mother's support, Sprinkles is reminded that she's a valuable member of the family and her feelings matter too.--Publisher.
Identifiers: ISBN: 979-8-9899915-6-3 (Paperback) | 979-8-9899915-7-0 (Hardcover) | LCCN: 2024911250
Subjects: LCSH: Autism in children--Juvenile literature. | Autistic children--Family relationships-- Juvenile literature. | Siblings--Juvenile literature. | Autism spectrum disorders in children --Juvenile literature. | CYAC: Autism. | Family life. | LCGFT: Picture books. | BISAC: FAMILY & RELATIONSHIPS / Autism Spectrum Disorders. | FAMILY & RELATIONSHIPS / Children with Special Needs. | PSYCHOLOGY / Psychopathology / Autism Spectrum Disorders.

Classification: LCC: RJ506.A9 M372 2024 | DDC: 616.85/882--dc23

Learn more about us at www.kidsspectrumstories.com

Kids Spectrum Stories

SPRINKLES
Has a Brother with Autism

Written by Jason Martinez and Emma Martinez
Illustrated by Eduardo Paj

Hi, my name is Sprinkles! I love to bake, paint, and spend time with my friends.

This is my brother, Chip.

Chip has autism and he gets really focused.

I love my brother, but there are times when I get frustrated. Sometimes it feels like my parents give him extra attention.

One day, Chip, my mom, and I went
to the grocery store to get ingredients for dinner.

At the store, Chip said that the music was
too loud and he kept walking away from us.

My mom followed him and said
"Chip, I need you to stay with us and be safe."

Chip started to blink and then he yelled.

I was really embarrassed and yelled back "Stop it Chip! You're making this hard!"

Chip froze for a moment and then started to cry.

My mom tried to help him calm down.

I was still upset.

When we got home, mom came into my room
and asked if I wanted to talk.

"It's not fair." I replied. "He always gets extra attention."

She reminded me,
"I'm here for you too. It's okay
to have big feelings.
Right now we are all learning
how to listen to our bodies,
Chip is learning about himself too."

I'm glad she was so patient with me.
"Thanks mom, I needed that" I said.

I came out of my room and found Chip playing with his cars.

"Chip, I'm sorry I got so upset. I know that you are trying your best."

Chip smiled and said "okay" quietly and went back to playing with his cars.

I was hoping for a different response.

But that's fine. I am learning how he communicates.

Mom suggested that we do an art project together.

It was something that we liked to do.
We both laughed as we made our silly paintings.

www.ingramcontent.com/pod-product-compliance
Lightning Source LLC
Chambersburg PA
CBHW041600260326

41914CB00011B/1330